Simple Machines

Screws

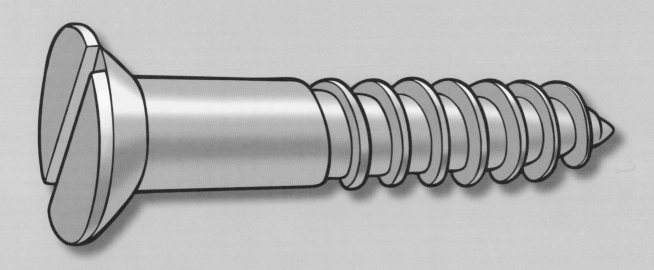

Chris Oxlade

W

FRANKLIN WATTS

LONDON • SYDNEY

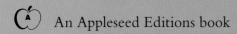 An Appleseed Editions book

First published in 2007 by Franklin Watts

Franklin Watts
338 Euston Road, London NW1 3BH

Franklin Watts Australia
Hachette Children's Books
Level 17/207 Kent St, Sydney, NSW 2000

© 2007 Appleseed Editions

Created by Appleseed Editions Ltd,
Well House, Friars Hill, Guestling,
East Sussex TN35 4ET

Designed by Helen James
Edited by Mary-Jane Wilkins
Artwork by Bill Donohoe

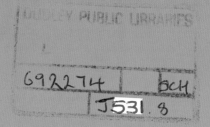
ISBN 978 0 7496 7568 4

Dewey Classification: 621.8' 82

A CIP catalogue for this book is available from the British Library

Photo credits
page 5 photo provided by permission from scienceshareware.com; 6 Lester Lefkowitz/
Corbis; 9 Krista Kennell/Zuma/Corbis; 11 Andrew Lambert Photography/Science Photo
Library; 12 Layne Kennedy/Corbis; 14 David Gallant/Corbis; 16 Jennie Woodcock;
Reflections Photolibrary/Corbis; 19 Alan Towse; Ecoscene/Corbis; 20 Deere & Company;
21 Martin Bond/Science Photo Library; 22 Underwood & Underwood/Corbis; 23 Time
Life Pictures/Getty Images; 28 Gehl Company/Corbis; 29 Krista Kennell/Zuma/Corbis

Printed in China

Franklin Watts is a division of Hachette Children's Books

Contents

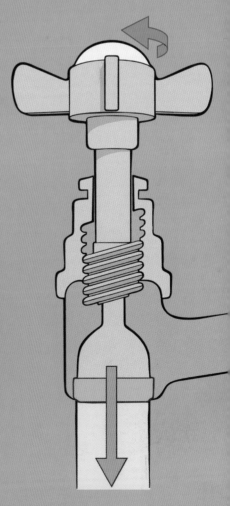

What is a simple machine?

A simple machine is something that helps you do a job. We use simple machines to help us every day. Here are some simple machines you might have at home.

door wedge

garden shears

door knob

wheelbarrow

This book is about simple machines
called screws. A nut is a type of screw.
We use nuts to join things together.
Corkscrews, woodscrews and drill bits
are screws, too.

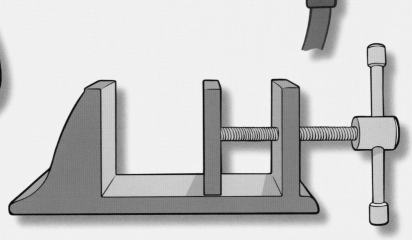

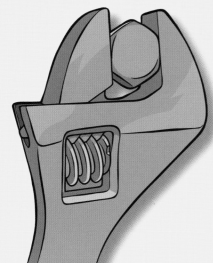

*Turning a screw
fixes the battery
cover to this toy.*

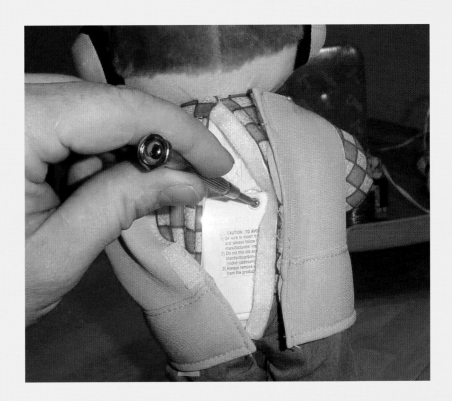

Pushes and pulls

You turn a screw to make it work. To turn it you push and pull on it. When you push and pull, the screw makes a push or pull too. Scientists call all pushes and pulls forces.

Pushing on the spanner turns the bolt. The bolt pulls on the nut.

We show pushes and pulls with arrows. The arrow points in the direction the force is pushing or pulling. The longer the arrow the bigger the push or pull is.

Red arrows show pushes and pulls.

Blue arrows show movement.

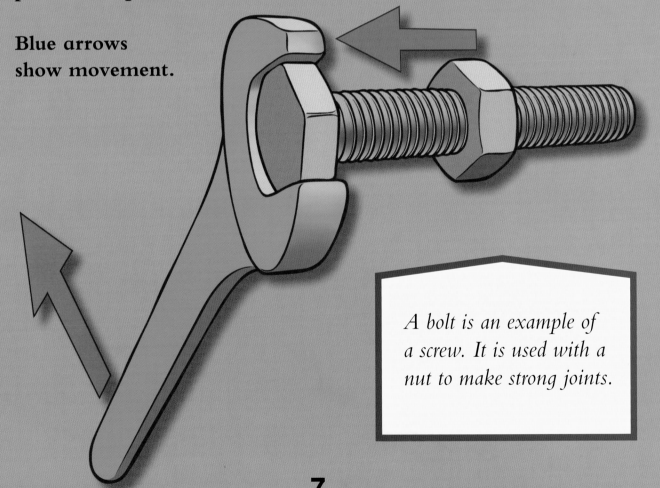

This force arrow shows that the person's feet are pushing down on the ground.

A bolt is an example of a screw. It is used with a nut to make strong joints.

How a screw works

A screw is a very simple machine. It is a rod with a spiral around the outside. The spiral is a screw thread. A screw only works when the thread presses against something.

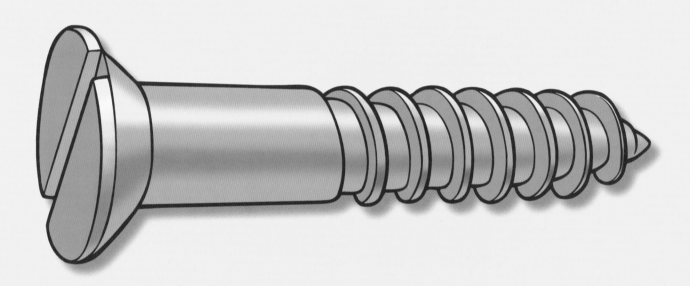

This is a simple screw. The thread goes around and around the outside, gradually going along the screw.

When you turn a screw, the thread pushes or pulls the material the screw is pressing against. This makes the screw move along.

Sometimes it makes the material move along instead. A small push or pull on the screw makes a large push or pull on the material.

Turning a bottle top gently makes it grip the bottle tightly.

Lifting with screws

We use screws to help lift heavy things. A screw jack is a machine for lifting up and supporting heavy objects. Turning the jack makes it rise out of the base.

When you turn the screw, the jack pushes the object upwards.

A scissor jack helps to lift up a car so the wheel can be changed.

The screw pulls the sides of the jack together. This pushes the top of the jack upwards.

Pushing and pulling makes the handle turn. This pushes the car upwards.

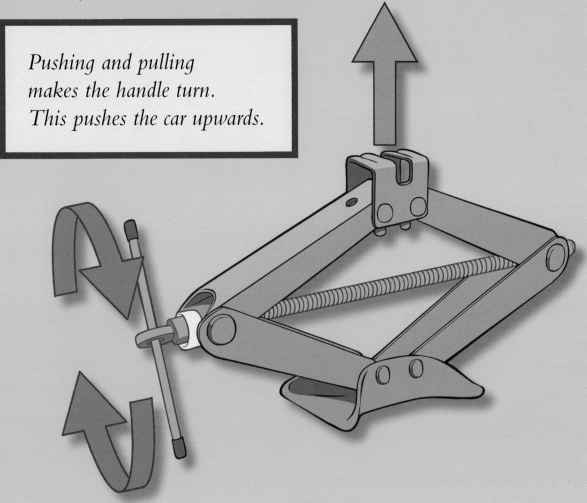

Gripping with screws

We use screws to grip things tightly.
We use a G-clamp for holding
objects together while we glue them.
A small bar helps to turn the screw.

*G-clamps press pieces
of wood together to make
a birch-bark canoe.*

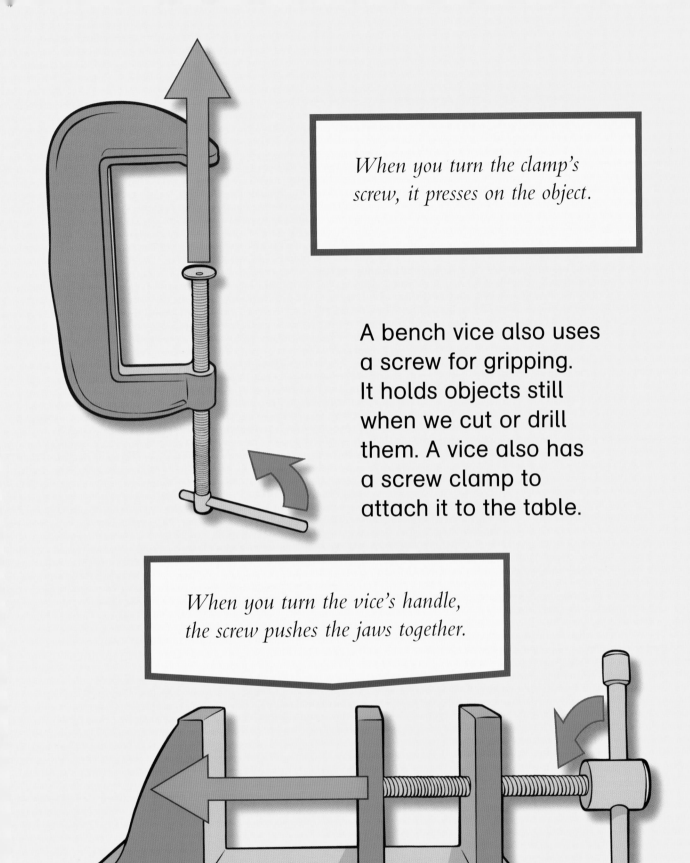

When you turn the clamp's screw, it presses on the object.

A bench vice also uses a screw for gripping. It holds objects still when we cut or drill them. A vice also has a screw clamp to attach it to the table.

When you turn the vice's handle, the screw pushes the jaws together.

Squeezing with screws

We use screws to squeeze things. A cider press squeezes the juice from apples.

The press has a large screw in the centre. Turning the handles makes a pad move down the screw on to the apples below.

A pull on the handles makes a larger push which crushes the apples.

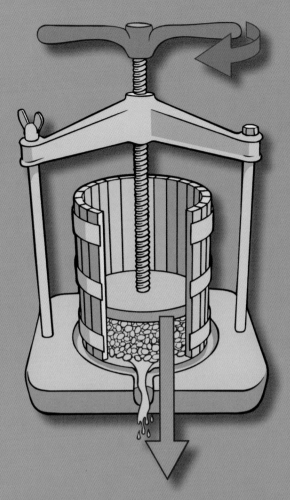

When you pull on the
handles, the pad presses
on the apples.

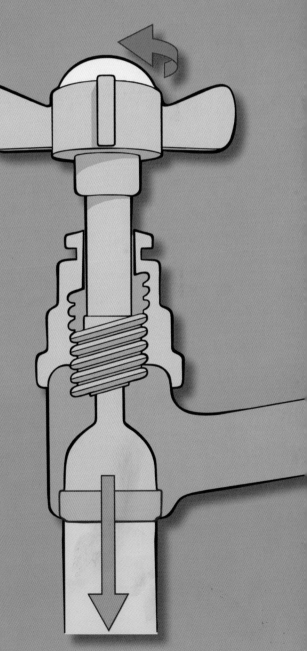

There is a rubber washer inside
a tap. Turning the tap handle
makes a screw squeeze the washer
against the end of the water pipe.
This stops the water flowing.

When you push on the tap
handle, the screw pushes
down on the washer.

Joining with screws

We use screws to join things together. A screw is a piece of metal with a sharp screw thread and a pointed end. It is used to join pieces of wood, plastic or metal.

Can you spot the bolts which help to hold this climbing frame together?

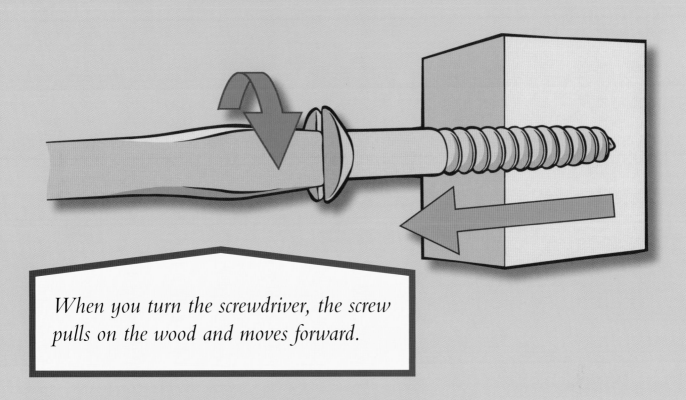

When you turn the screwdriver, the screw pulls on the wood and moves forward.

A nut and bolt are used to join pieces of material together. The screw threads on the nut and bolt slot into each other. When the nut is turned, it pulls on the bolt.

When the nut turns it pulls on the bolt.

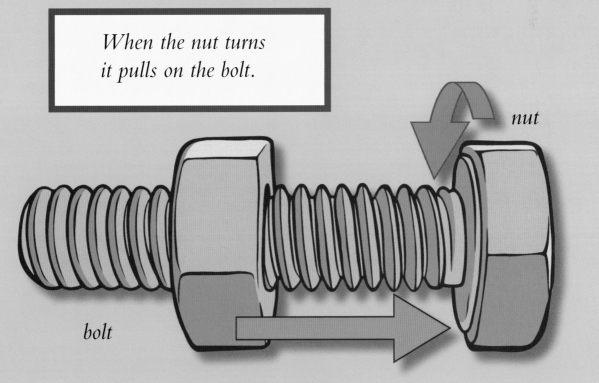

nut

bolt

Moving with screws

We use screws to move materials from place to place. A drill bit for drilling wood and brick has a screw thread.

The cutting blades of the drill break off small bits of material. As the drill bit turns, the screw thread moves waste materials from the hole.

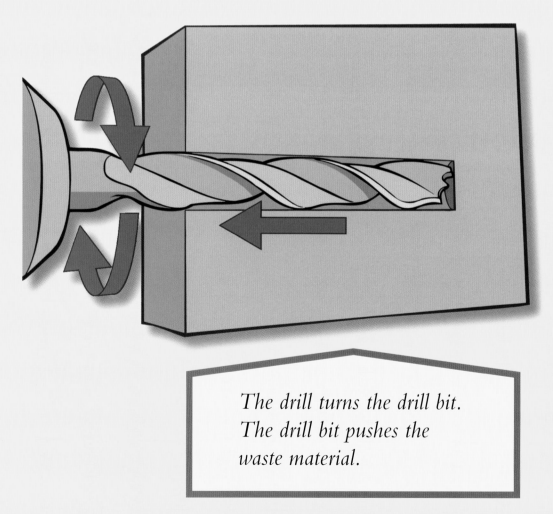

The drill turns the drill bit. The drill bit pushes the waste material.

A machine called a screw conveyor moves materials in factories. Inside is a screw with a wide thread. As the screw turns, material is trapped by the thread and pushed along.

This screw conveyor is moving plastics through a recycling plant. Can you see the screw thread?

A motor turns the screw. The screw pushes the material along.

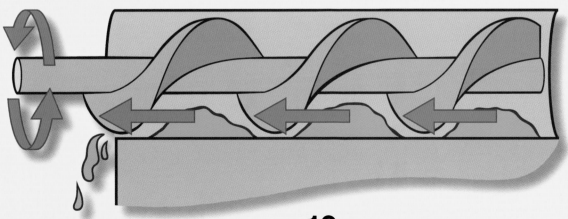

Screws in machines

Complicated machines often use screws to work.

A combine harvester cuts down crops and separates the grain from the stalks. A screw at the front of the machine collects the crop.

The screw moves the cut crop sideways.

An adjustable spanner can be used on nuts of any size. It has a screw that moves the jaws together to grip the nut.

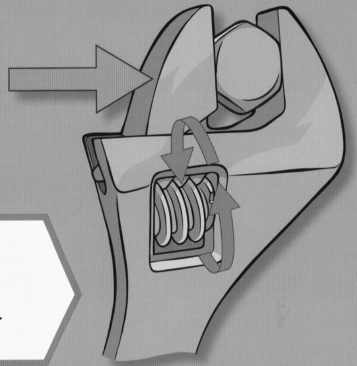

You can adjust the spanner's jaws with one finger. The spanner grips the nut tightly.

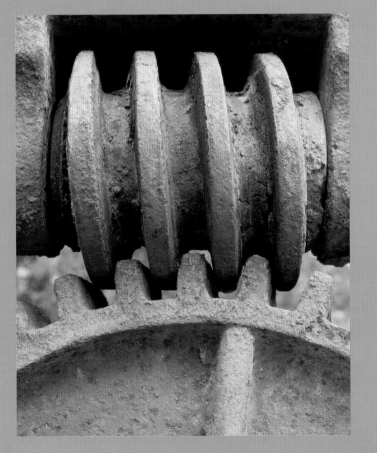

A worm gear is a special type of gear that uses a screw. This motor has a worm gear. It makes the wheels turn slowly.

When the screw turns quickly, the wheel turns slowly.

Screws in the past

People have been using screws for thousands of years.

The printing press was invented more than 500 years ago. The large wooden screw presses inky metal letters on to paper to print pages for a book.

Can you see the giant screw that works this press?

Romans watching an Archimedean screw lifting water.

This is an Archimedean screw. It was invented thousands of years ago to raise water from rivers into fields to water crops.

The screw conveyor on page 19 is a modern version of this simple machine.

Fun with screws

On the next four pages are some activities for you to do. They will help you to understand how screws work.

A MODEL SCREW JACK

You will need:
• a large nut and bolt (you could use a nut and bolt from a model construction kit)
• an old CD
• some modelling clay or sticky tape

| 1 | Put the nut over the hole in the middle of the CD. |

| 2 | Attach the nut to the CD with modelling clay or sticky tape. |

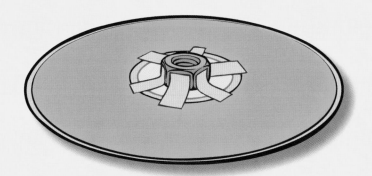

| 3 | Put the CD flat on a table with the nut underneath. |

| 4 | Screw the bolt slowly into the nut while you hold the CD. |

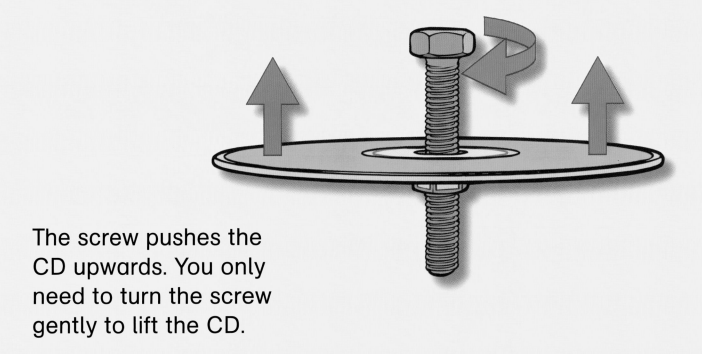

The screw pushes the CD upwards. You only need to turn the screw gently to lift the CD.

A SCREW CONVEYOR

You will need:
- a pencil
- a piece of thin rope about 40 cm long
- sticky tape
- thin card (about 15 cm x 8 cm)
- small dried beans or peas

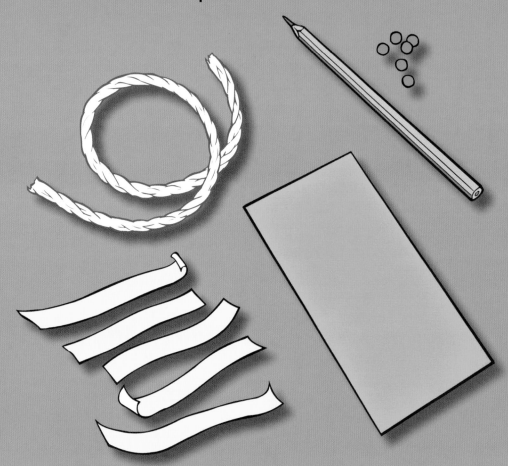

<table>
<tr><td>

1

</td><td>

Tape one end of the rope to one end of the pencil.

</td></tr>
</table>

2 Wrap the rope tightly round the pencil.
Spread the coils of rope along the pencil.
Tape the rope to the other end of the pencil.

3 Wrap a piece of card around
the pencil and rope.

4 Drop some small dried
beans into the card tube.

Twist the pencil round.
The screw pushes the beans along the tube.

Spot the screws

Can you spot all the screws
on these pages? Try to work
out what each screw does.

Can you see
the screw here?
What does it do?

These screws are
inside an electric plug.
What do they grip?

Answers are on page 32.

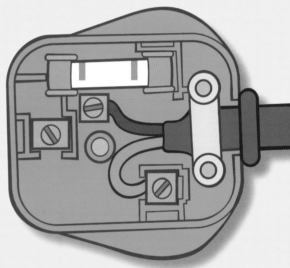

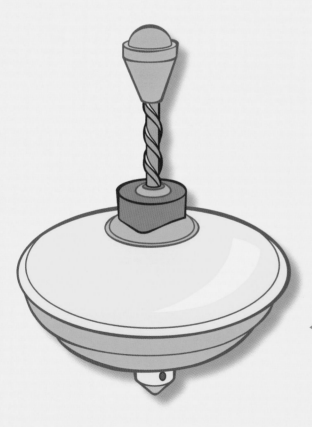

Where is the screw
thread in this toy?

Words to remember

Archimedean screw
A tube with a screw inside that lifts water uphill when it is turned.

bench vice
A machine attached to a bench that is used to grip objects tightly while they are cut.

drill bit
A rod with a sharp blade at one end and a screw along its sides, that is turned to drill holes.

forces
Pushes or pulls.

G-clamp
A clamp shaped like a capital letter G, that uses a screw to hold two pieces of material together.

screw conveyor
A machine that uses a screw thread
to move loose or runny materials
from place to place.

screw jack
A machine that uses a screw to lift
heavy objects upwards.

screw thread
The groove around a bolt or screw.

spanner
A lever used to turn a nut or bolt washer.
An adjustable spanner can turn different
sized nuts and bolts.

worm gear
A screw and a gear wheel together.
When the screw turns fast, it makes
the wheel turn slowly.

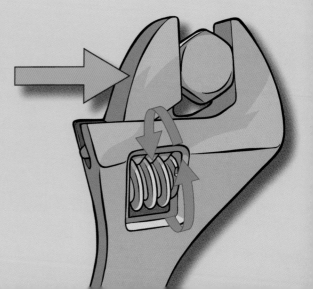

Index

Answers to pages 28-29

The screw is called an auger. It digs up earth.
This is a corkscrew for taking a cork out of a bottle.
You can see the ends of three screws. They grip wires.
The screw is near the top. It makes the top spin when you press down.